AF228298

Lerner SPORTS

MEET SABRINA IONESCU

MARGARET J. GOLDSTEIN

Lerner Publications ◆ Minneapolis

Lerner Publications Company
An imprint of Lerner Publishing Group, Inc.
241 First Avenue North
Minneapolis, MN 55401 USA

For reading levels and more information, look up this title at www.lernerbooks.com.

Main body text set in Aptifer Slab LT Pro. Typeface provided by Linotype AG.

Editor: Matt Doeden

Library of Congress Cataloging-in-Publication Data

Names: Goldstein, Margaret J., author.
Title: Meet Sabrina Ionescu : New York liberty superstar / Margaret J. Goldstein.
Description: Minneapolis, MN : Lerner Publications, [2024] | Series: Sports VIPs (Lerner sports) | Includes bibliographical references and index. | Audience: Ages 7–11 | Audience: Grades 4–6 | Summary: "Sabrina Ionescu was an all-time great college basketball player. In the WNBA, she overcame a serious ankle injury to become a star with the New York Liberty. See why fans are so excited about Ionescu"— Provided by publisher.
Identifiers: LCCN 2022049974 (print) | LCCN 2022049975 (ebook) | ISBN 9781728490922 (library binding) | ISBN 9798765603956 (paperback) | ISBN 9798765601235 (ebook)
Subjects: LCSH: Ionescu, Sabrina, 1997– —Juvenile literature. | Women basketball players—United States—Biography—Juvenile literature. | Guards (Basketball)—United States—Biography—Juvenile literature. | New York Liberty (Basketball team)—Juvenile literature. | BISAC: JUVENILE NONFICTION / Biography & Autobiography / Sports & Recreation
Classification: LCC GV884.I66 G65 2024 (print) | LCC GV884.I66 (ebook) | DDC 796.323092 [B]— dc23/eng/20221019

LC record available at https://lccn.loc.gov/2022049974
LC ebook record available at https://lccn.loc.gov/2022049975

Manufactured in the United States of America
1-53023-51041-2/14/2023

TABLE OF CONTENTS

DRAFT DAY

The 2020 Women's National Basketball Association (WNBA) Draft was not a normal draft. There were no crowds, no camera crews, and no bright lights or loud music. The COVID-19 pandemic had forced the draft to take place remotely. Sabrina Ionescu sat in her living room in Walnut Creek, California. Her family surrounded her. Everyone focused on a camera and TV monitor set up in front of them.

FAST FACTS

DATE OF BIRTH: December 6, 1997

POSITION: guard

LEAGUE: Women's National Basketball Association

PROFESSIONAL HIGHLIGHTS: chosen first in the 2020 WNBA draft; had the first triple-double in New York Liberty history; was the first WNBA player with more than 500 points, more than 200 rebounds, and more than 200 assists in one season

PERSONAL HIGHLIGHTS: has a twin brother; was friends with Kobe Bryant and spoke at his memorial service; earned a degree in social sciences from the University of Oregon

Ionescu became a top WNBA prospect during her college career.

Ionescu had been looking forward to this moment since childhood. The time came for the first draft pick. WNBA commissioner Cathy Engelbert read the selection: "With the first pick in the 2020 WNBA Draft, the New York Liberty select Sabrina Ionescu from the University of Oregon."

Ionescu's family cheered. Her parents gave her big hugs. She was headed to New York City to play professional basketball.

Later, a reporter asked Ionescu how it felt to be the number-one draft pick. She replied, "I'm just really blessed to be in this position that I've worked so hard for my entire life." At last, she was headed to the WNBA.

Ionescu became an instant fan favorite. Here she poses with a fan before a 2022 WNBA playoff game.

TEAM SPIRIT

Sabrina Ionescu and her twin brother, Eddy, were born on December 6, 1997, in Walnut Creek, California. Sabrina and Eddy were close. Sabrina called them "built-in best friends." Their parents, Liliana Blaj and Dan Ionescu, were immigrants from Romania, a nation in Eastern Europe. The twins' big brother, Andrei, was nine when they were born.

When Sabrina was three, she played with a basketball for the first time. She loved the sport. So did Eddy. When they got older, the twins played basketball for hours at home or at nearby Larkey Park. They often played rough, trying to outdo each other.

Ionescu, pictured here in 2015, was a star at Miramonte High School in California.

Andrei and other kids often joined them on the court. Most of the boys were older and taller than Sabrina. She had to learn to be tough. Boys often wouldn't pass to her, so she learned to be a great rebounder so she could get her hands on the ball. She also focused on passing. That made her a valued teammate.

Ionescu tries to evade defender Aisia Robertson during a 2013 Miramonte High School game.

In fourth grade, Sabrina joined a non-school girls' basketball team called the Cal Stars. Sabrina's middle school did not have a girls' basketball team. Her family asked the school district if she could join the boys' team. But the district said no. So Sabrina started a girls' team. She also played with Eddy's non-school team when they needed a player.

CHAPTER 2

GRADE A

In 2012, Sabrina started attending Miramonte High School in Orinda, California. She joined the girls' basketball team. Under coach Kelly Sopak, the team was already good. Sabrina made it even better. The team went 27–3 during her freshman year.

In the summer of 2013, Sabrina tried out for USA Basketball, which runs US national teams. She made the U16 (under age sixteen) girls' team, and the next summer she played on the U17 team. Both teams won gold at international championships.

Sabrina continued to play with the Cal Stars, which won the Nike Elite Youth Basketball League girls' championship in 2015. The Cal Stars also ran camps for young basketball players. Sabrina worked as a coach, helping younger girls improve their games.

During Sabrina's four years of high school ball, Miramonte went 119–9. In her senior year, she averaged 25.3 points, 8.8 assists, and 7.6 rebounds per game. In all

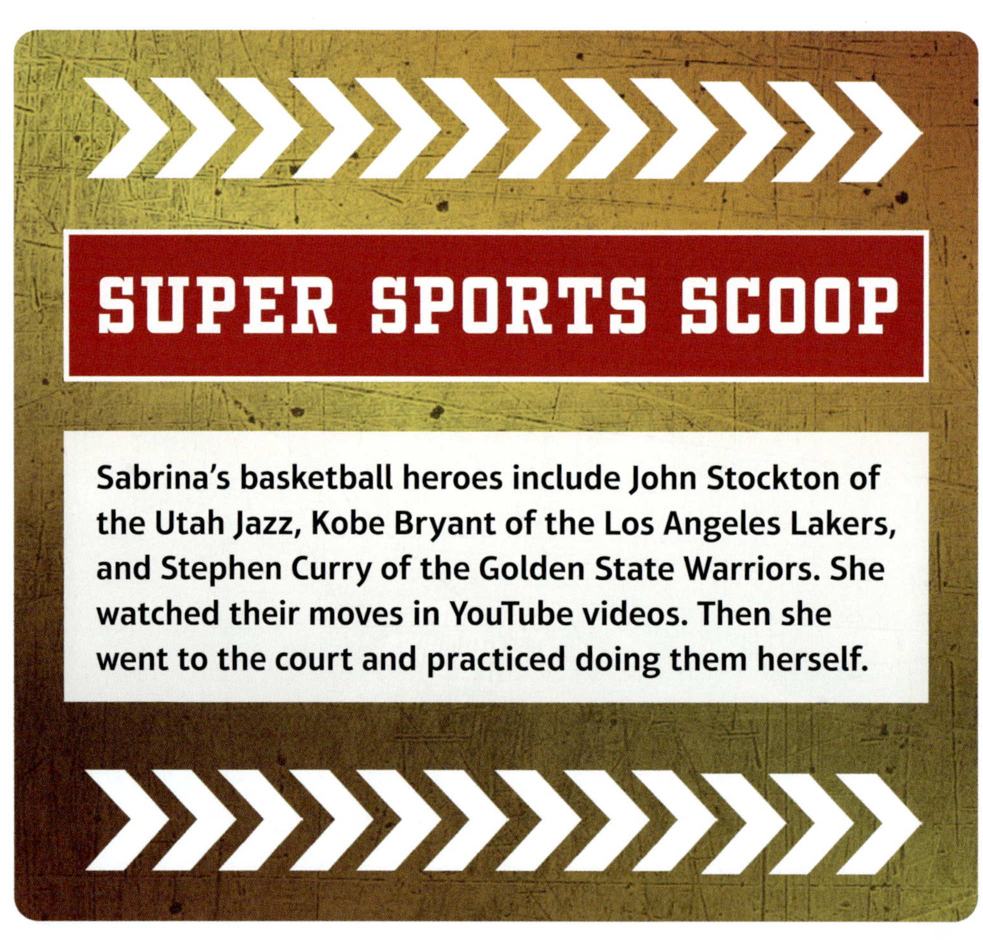

Sabrina's basketball heroes include John Stockton of the Utah Jazz, Kobe Bryant of the Los Angeles Lakers, and Stephen Curry of the Golden State Warriors. She watched their moves in YouTube videos. Then she went to the court and practiced doing them herself.

Ionescu starred for the West team in the 2016 McDonald's All-American Game. She scored 25 points in the victory.

four years combined, she scored 2,606 points. It was a school record.

In 2016, Sabrina finished her senior year at Miramonte. The honors came rolling in. She was chosen to play in the McDonald's All-American Game, an all-star game for the nation's best high school players. She scored 25 points, including seven three-pointers, to lead her West team to a 97–88 victory over the East. She was named the game's Most Valuable Player. She also earned several Player of the Year honors.

Coach Sopak praised Sabrina as she prepared to graduate. "Heck, who does not want to coach a kid that is talented, works hard and will not accept losing? Sabrina is a big-time player but all she cares about is her team and that they win. The awards . . . and records, they don't mean anything to her. She just wants to win and that's a very special quality in a player."

Around the country, women's college basketball coaches wanted Sabrina on their teams. Top basketball schools offered her scholarships. Sabrina wanted to stay close to home. She liked Kelly Graves, head coach of the University of Oregon Ducks. She chose to join his squad in Eugene, Oregon.

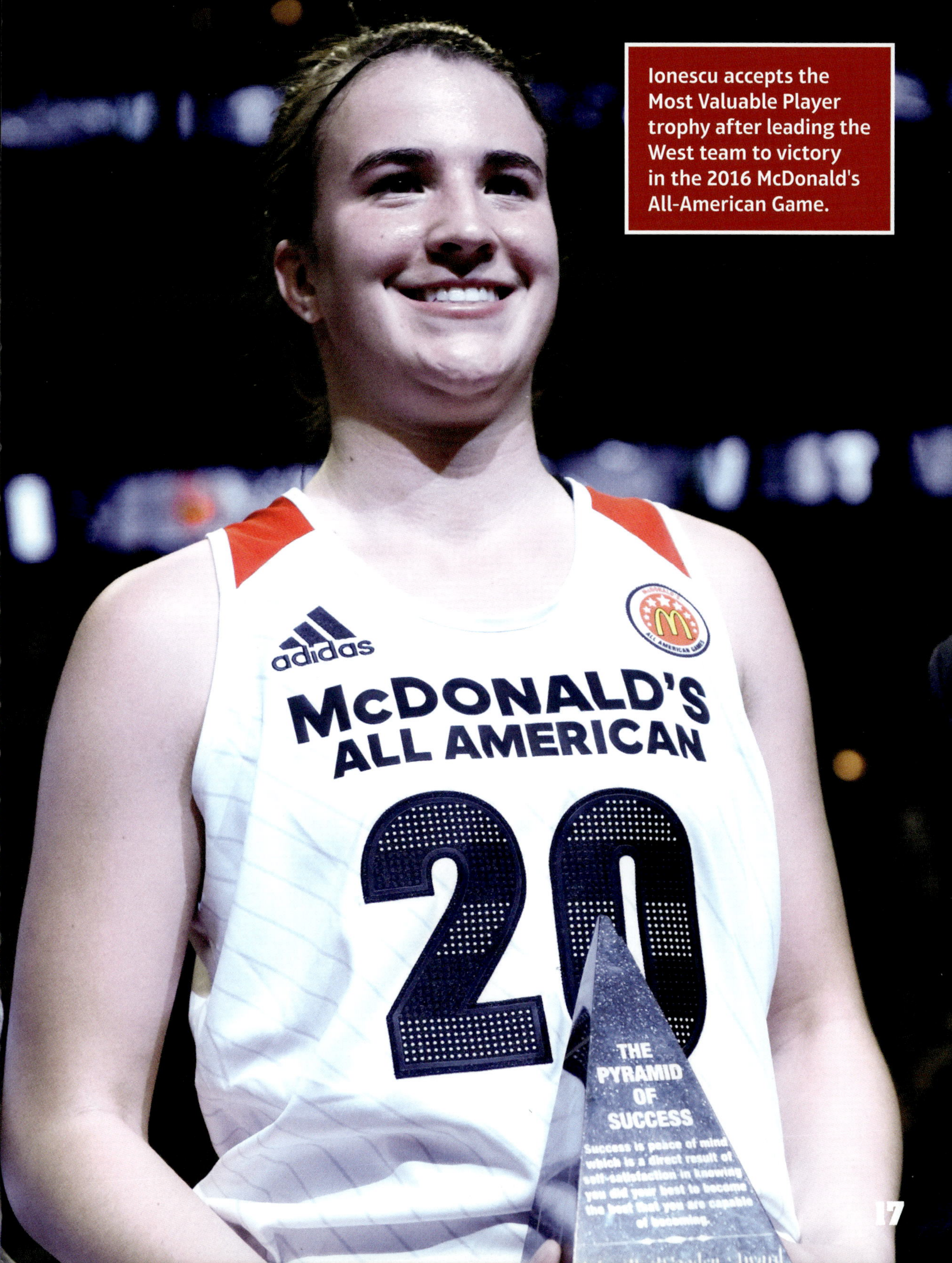

Ionescu accepts the Most Valuable Player trophy after leading the West team to victory in the 2016 McDonald's All-American Game.

QUEEN OF THE TRIPLE-DOUBLES

At Oregon, Ionescu lived up to her promise. Many basketball players excel at one aspect of the game: scoring, rebounding, passing, blocking, or stealing. Ionescu did it all. In the seventh game of the Ducks' 2016–2017 season, against San Jose State, she posted her first triple-double with 11 points, 12 rebounds, and 11 assists.

The Ducks dominated. Ionescu was known as the triple-double queen. She posted four in her freshman year, six as a sophomore, and eight as a junior.

In 2017, Oregon made the National Collegiate Athletic Association (NCAA) Tournament, nicknamed March Madness. Ionescu and her teammates made a run to the Elite Eight, where they lost to Connecticut. They reached the Elite Eight again the following year. This time they lost to Notre Dame.

Defenders close in on Ionescu during a 2017 NCAA Tournament game versus the Maryland Terrapins.

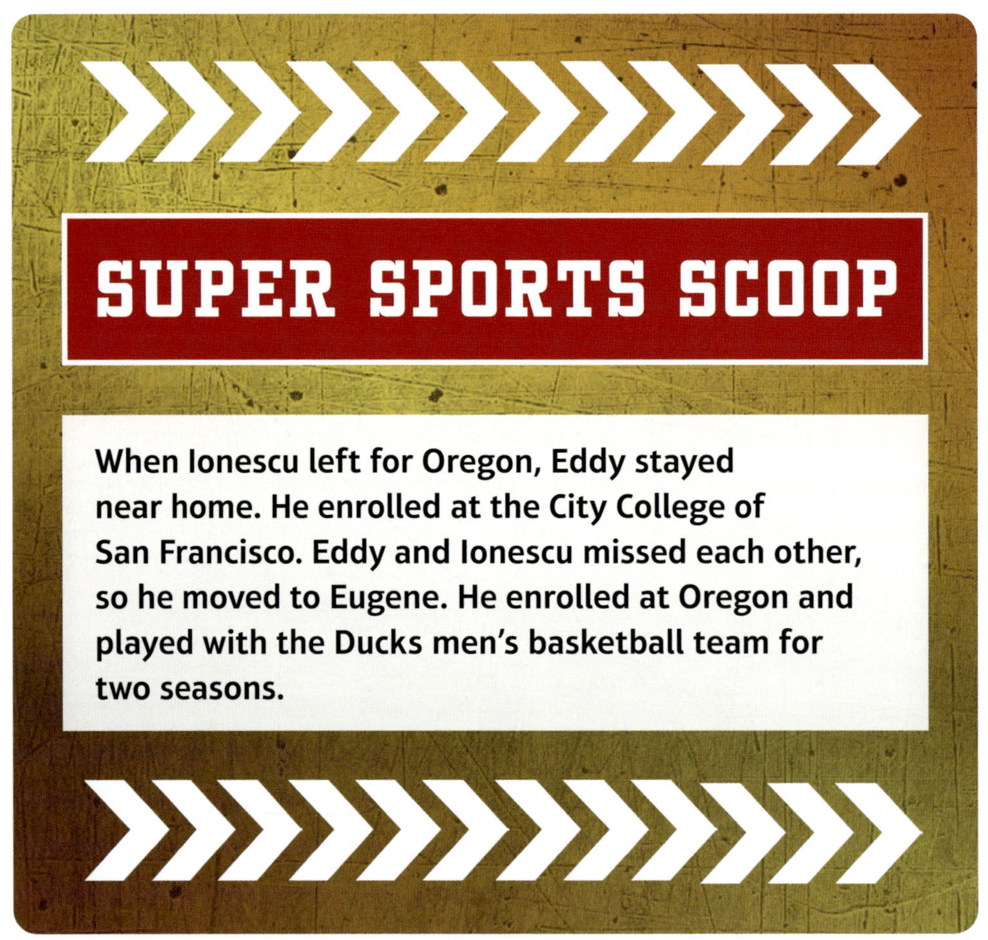

Oregon had many strong players. They included Satou Sabally and Ruthy Hebard. But Ionescu was the brightest star. At a Golden State Warriors game, she met Stephen Curry, who called her the "walking Triple Dub." At another game, she met Kobe Bryant and his teenage daughter Gianna, who was also a basketball standout. Sabrina and Kobe became friends.

At the 2019 NCAA tournament, Oregon reached the Elite Eight again. They beat the tough Mississippi State Bulldogs by a score of 88–84. The Ducks were headed to their first Final Four. They were just two wins away from the NCAA championship.

But their run ended there. The Baylor Lady Bears shut down Ionescu and Oregon's other shooters. The Lady Bears took the game 72–67.

Ionescu sets Oregon's offense during their 2019 Final Four game against Baylor.

Ionescu could have skipped her senior year of college and gone right to the WNBA. But she wanted to take the Ducks to another Final Four. She wanted a chance to win it all. She wrote in the online Players' Tribune, "I couldn't be happier to announce that I'm coming back to the University of Oregon for the 2019–2020 basketball season."

Ionescu and her teammates celebrate a victory over Stanford in February 2020.

CHAPTER 4

LIFE AND LIBERTY

Ionescu's senior year at Oregon began as expected, with her team winning big. In the classroom, she studied business branding. She focused on building her own brand as an athlete. But life turned dark in the winter of 2020. Kobe and Gianna Bryant died in a helicopter crash. Ionescu was devastated.

More bad news followed. COVID-19 was spreading. People around the world were getting sick. Many were dying. The NCAA canceled March Madness to avoid spreading the illness.

Ionescu finished her college career with 26 triple-doubles. It was an NCAA record for both men and women. She was also the first player in NCAA history with 2,000 career points, 1,000 career rebounds, and 1,000 career assists.

Ionescu started her WNBA career with the New York Liberty in the summer of 2020. In her third game, she suffered an ankle injury. She had to sit out the rest of the season.

In 2021, Ionescu had the first triple-double in Liberty history. In 2022, she became the first WNBA player to score more than 500 points, grab more than 200 rebounds, and dish out more than 200 assists in one year.

Ionescu joined the Liberty for her rookie season in 2020. An ankle injury cut her season short.

One of her best games took place on July 6, 2022. Ionescu drilled shots from all over the court against the Las Vegas Aces. She scored 31 points on her way to another triple-double. The Liberty won the game, 116–107.

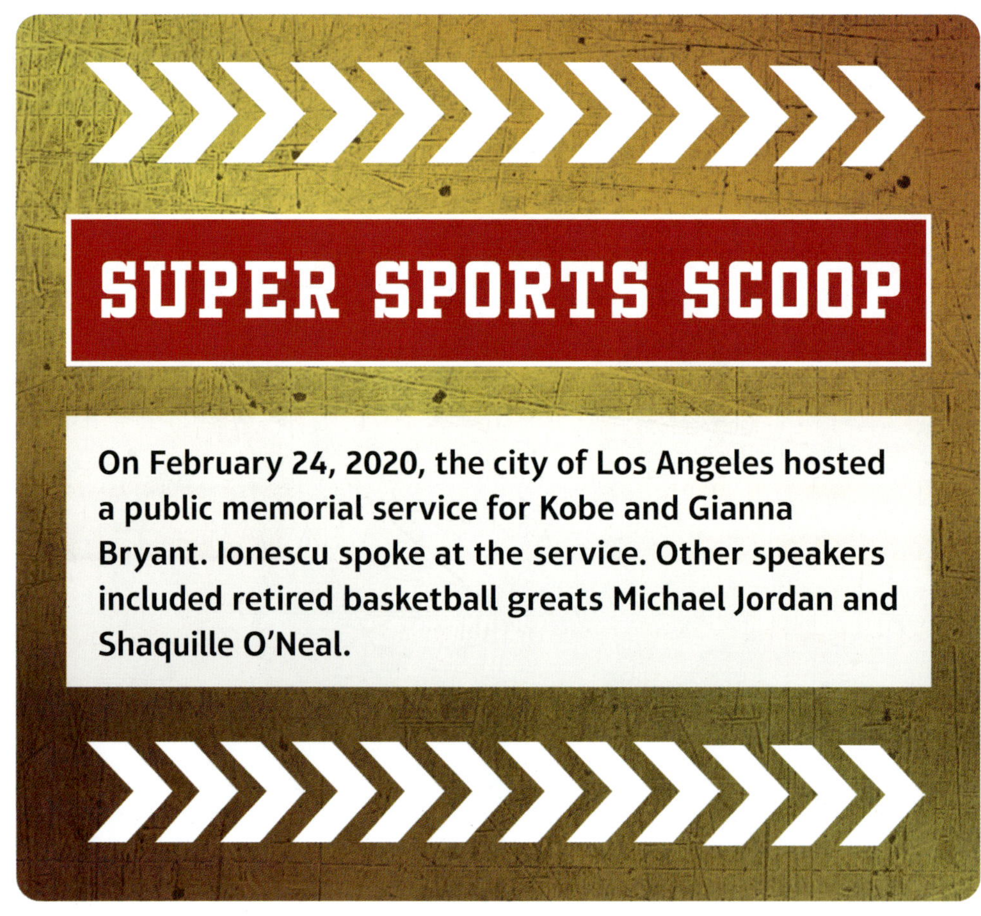

On February 24, 2020, the city of Los Angeles hosted a public memorial service for Kobe and Gianna Bryant. Ionescu spoke at the service. Other speakers included retired basketball greats Michael Jordan and Shaquille O'Neal.

Ionescu rasies her arms in celebration after the Liberty defeated the Chicago Sky in a 2022 playoff game.

The Liberty faced the Chicago Sky in the 2022 WNBA Playoffs. Ionescu scored 22 points in the first game. She led New York to victory. But Chicago came back to win the next two games. New York's season was over. Ionescu was disappointed with the loss. But she had given New York fans plenty of reasons to hope for a bright future.

SABRINA IONESCU CAREER STATS

GAMES:
69

FIELD GOALS:
343

FREE THROWS:
203

ASSISTS:
423

REBOUNDS:
438

STEALS:
59

BLOCKS:
26

Stats are accurate through the 2022 WNBA regular season.

GLOSSARY

branding: the promotion of a product, company, or person using advertising, logos, social media, and other media

COVID-19: an infectious disease that emerged in late 2019 and spread around the world

draft: a system for selecting new players to professional sports teams

Elite Eight: at the NCAA Tournament, eight teams that have won three earlier rounds of single-elimination play and that pair off to determine which teams go to the Final Four

Final Four: at the NCAA Tournament, four teams that have won four early rounds of single-elimination play and that pair off to determine which two teams play for the championship

guard: a player stationed in the backcourt, away from the basket, who directs team play

immigrant: a person who leaves one nation to settle in another

remotely: from a distance, using computers and other communications technology to connect people

scholarship: money given to a student to help pay for their education

triple-double: having double-digit totals in three categories out of five (points, rebounds, assists, blocks, and steals) in a single game

SOURCE NOTES

6　Matthew Loves Ball, "WNBA 2020 Draft Highlights," YouTube, April 18, 2020, https://www.youtube.com/watch?v=wkNW2q PQyBQ

7　ESPN, "Sabrina Ionescu Selected No. 1 Overall by the New York Liberty in WNBA Draft," YouTube, April 17, 2020, https://www.youtube.com/watch?v=47b0cHRQpOA

8　Maria Taylor, "The Legend of Sabrina Ionescu," ESPN, March 16, 2020, https://www.espn.com/espn/feature/story/_/id/28878754/the-legend-sabrina-ionescu

16　Harold Abend, "Sabrina Ionescu: Gatorade Player of the Year Is Complete Package," Prep2Prep, March 10, 2016, https://www.prep2prep.com/feature.aspx?articleID=9781

20　Tamryn Spruill, "Steph Curry hangs with 'walking Triple Dub' Sabrina Ionescu," WarriorsWire, December 30, 2018, https://warriorswire.usatoday.com/2018/12/30/steph-curry-hangs-with-walking-triple-dub-sabrina-ionescu/

22　Sabrina Ionescu, "A Letter to Ducks Nation," Players' Tribune, April 7, 2019, https://www.theplayerstribune.com/articles/sabrina-ionescu-oregon-basketball

LEARN MORE

Doeden, Matt. *G.O.A.T. Women's Basketball Teams*. Minneapolis: Lerner Publications, 2021.

Ducksters: Basketball
https://www.ducksters.com/sports/basketball.php

The New York Liberty
https://liberty.wnba.com

Scheff, Matt. *NBA and WNBA Finals: Basketball's Biggest Playoffs.* Minneapolis: Lerner Publications, 2021.

Sports Illustrated Kids: Basketball
https://www.sikids.com/basketball

Whiting, Jim. *The Story of the New York Liberty*. Mankato, MN: Creative Education, 2023.

INDEX

PHOTO ACKNOWLEDGMENTS

Image credits: AP Photo/Sean D. Eliot/The Day, p. 4; Tim Clayton/Corbis/ Getty Images, p. 6; Michael Reaves/Getty Images, p. 7; Jose Carlos Fajardo/ MediaNews Group/The Mercury News/Getty Images, p. 8; Dan Honda/ MediaNews Group/The Mercury News/Getty Images, p. 9; Doug Duran/ MediaNews Group/The Mercury News/Getty Images, pp. 10, 13; AP Photo/Matt Marton, pp. 12, 15; David Banks/Getty Images, p.17; Joseph Weiser/Icon Sportswire/Getty Images, p. 18; Tim Clayton/Corbis/Getty Images, p. 19; AP Photo/Chris O'Meara, p. 21; AP Photo/ Cody Glenn/ Icon Sportswire, p. 22; David Dennis/Icon Sportswire/Getty Images, p. 23; Alika Jenner/Getty Images, p. 24; Julio Aguilar/Getty Images, p. 25; Melissa Tamez/Icon Sportswire/Getty Images, p. 27.

Cover: AP Photo/Mark Baker.